CERAMIC SKILLBOOKS

Series Editor
Murray Fieldhouse

Slipware

John Pollex

PITMAN/WATSON-GUPTILL

PITMAN PUBLISHING LIMITED
39 Parker Street, London WC2B 5PB

Associated Companies
Copp Clark Pitman, Toronto
Pitman Publishing New Zealand Ltd, Wellington
Pitman Publishing Pty Ltd, Melbourne

First published in Great Britain by Pitman Publishing Ltd 1979
Published in the USA by Watson-Guptill Publications 1979

© Pitman Publishing 1979

WATSON-GUPTILL PUBLICATIONS
a division of Billboard Publications Inc.,
1515 Broadway, New York, NY 10036

UK ISBN 0 273 01185 5 (cased edition)
UK ISBN 0 273 01188 X (paperback edition)
US ISBN 8230—4857—8

Text set in 10/12 pt IBM Century, printed and bound in Great Britain
at The Pitman Press, Bath

Contents

Acknowledgements

My first teachers at Sir John Cass — Carol Steward, Ray Bone, Boyd Parker. Victor Margrie and the staff at Harrow from 1968 to 1970. Bryan Newman for my first job as assistant. Colin Pearson for my second job, and for being much more than an employer. My past assistants, John Paltridge, Richard Godfrey, Hugh Perry, Ian Lister, Nan Musgrove. Special thanks to my present assistant, Graham Stevens, to my editors Cathy Gosling and Susan Harley, and photographers David Lewis and John Bagulay.

Dedication

Dedicated to Alan and Evelyn Shave, and Pamela.

Fig. 1 Large thrown dish, 21 inches diameter, trailed decoration. Note how the small white dots seem to illuminate the pattern.

Introduction

Before introducing you to slipware, I would like to offer some thoughts and observations I have made during the time I have been a potter.

For several years before I started making pots, I was very interested in Eastern religions and philosophy — Zen Buddhism in particular. I was looking for a path to self-discovery or self-knowledge, which at the time had very few practical outlets.

A friend advised me to enrol for pottery classes, which I did. Soon after this I was at the Victoria and Albert Museum where Bernard Leach was giving a lecture. I remember him saying that nearly all the Japanese arts and crafts are Zen based. This was what I wanted to hear, and with no idea what the future would bring, I began a life as a potter. Today I am just as excited by making and decorating pots as I was at the beginning.

Which aspect of pottery you decide to study will depend on your feelings and thoughts. At present these are invisible, but they will come to life as you interpret them through the practical disciplines which the clay and the techniques you use will impose on you. You will also be faced with the limitations of your experience of pottery.

It seems to me that when we begin anything new, one of the things we fear most is making a mistake. This sense of failure or fear immediately inhibits the free flow of feelings into our work and life. It is essential to give up this attitude and come to terms with ourselves and our limitations.

A study of children's work will soon indicate what I mean. The young child's mind does not yet know the meaning of failure and is free to explore the medium in which it is working — or

Fig. 2 Commemorative dish, 28
inches diameter. This dish celebrates
the twenty-first anniversary of the
Devon Guild of Craftsmen. It
combines a trailed rim with a
sgraffito centre. The coat of arms
is that of the county of Devon.

should I say playing. Hence the freedom and spontaneity of children's work and the enjoyment they show in doing it.

Clay wants to know you as much as you should want to know and understand the clay. After all, it has been in the ground for millions of years, waiting for you to come along, so it has a lot to tell you about itself and yourself. As the saying goes, 'Our pots are made of what we potters are'. You must have respect for the clay and materials you use. If you do not, you may be surprised when you find out who is in control.

I would like to say something here about the way we look at pots. If we compare one pot with another, it suggests that one is better than the other; the act of looking then becomes divided. Each pot is an expression of the moment in time it was made, and therefore has the truth of that moment contained within it. To see *that* truth is all that is necessary when looking at a pot. Immediately you see it, you are free then to look freshly at the next pot.

I have been asked if I get bored repeating the same pattern, or throwing a batch of pots all the same shape. I have to reply 'no' — each one is subtly different. Each one stands forward as itself and can be seen free from the ugliness of comparison.

What has this got to do with slipware? The very nature and substance of slip is its flow. I have always wanted to understand the flow and rhythms within life and myself. Decorating pots with slip invites you to open up to yourself so that the slip will flow freely. It is from this invitation accepted with love and interest that you can eventually begin to flow a little within yourself.

1 What is slipware?

Slipware is usually an earthenware body that has been decorated with liquid clay known as slip. It is applied in varying consistencies to all forms of pottery in many different ways. Most slips are made from the clay body used in the pot with colouring added for contrast. After decoration has been done, the ware is given a transparent lead glaze to give a very shiny finish.

Making slipware needs a lot of patience, a steady hand and enough time for the job not to be hurried. The most common slip decoration methods are trailing, sgraffito, feathering, marbling and combing. I use all these techniques to produce very different results. Each one of them offers the potter scope for imaginative design and the opportunity to bring out the best qualities in a piece of work through the richness of slip as a decorative medium.

Slipware was introduced to this country from The Netherlands during the late sixteenth and early seventeenth centuries, although it probably had its origin in the Far East. Shards of pottery covered with slip and said to be five thousand years old have been excavated in Kyushu, South Japan. The Romans also decorated pots with slip.

It was in Staffordshire that the English tradition was born. The seventeenth-century Staffordshire potters were quick to discover the many and varied uses of slip for decorating their pots. What could be more natural than to decorate clay pots with clay itself? Soon after this, slipware began to be made in different parts of the country, particularly in the counties of Kent, Sussex, Somerset and Devon.

The pots that were produced during this period were nearly all for a domestic purpose — platters, jugs, bowls, dishes etc. There

Fig. 3 Salt kit or pig, probably made at Whetherhills Pottery, Yorkshire. This pot was decorated by putting white slip directly on to the body which would have made the decorating easier as the pot was probably held by placing the free hand inside the pot while decorating with the other. There was no background slip to be damaged by handling. However, slip does not flow as easily when applied directly on to the body as it does when applied to a background slip unless the pot is dampened first. Judging by the confident flow of the lines, I imagine that this pot was decorated swiftly.

Fig. 4 Puzzle jug. The thick rim is hollow with three spouts from which you are supposed to drink. But below the rim, in the neck of the jug, holes have been cut to make this impossible — unless you know the secret!

Fig. 5 Detail of puzzle jug.

were also some very ingenious pots made at that time such as beetle-traps, salt-kits, puzzle jugs, whistles and money box pots.

Slipware inscriptions are a distinctive feature and many of them record, in a small way, the history of the period. Rhymes were also plentifully inscribed, particularly on harvest jugs where the verse usually suggested that nothing could be better than good ale poured from a well-made jug and drunk after a thirsty spell of harvesting.

Appreciating the work of the early (English) slipware potters is obviously the best way to start your own efforts at slip decoration. Their achievements should not be forgotten, neither should the love and care which went into their pots. Chapter 6 tells you

Fig. 6 *Left*: a water sprinkler from Donyatt, $8\frac{1}{2}$ inches tall, made in 1661. The decoration is trailed on a green slip. The inscription reads 'James Choncee. Pott 1661'. *Right*: a money box, $10\frac{1}{2}$ inches, early 18th century.
Both are in the *Plymouth City Museum*
Photo: John Baguley

where to go to see some examples of early slipware.

I hope this book will offer you an insight into the possibilities of using slip as a means of decorating pots, and also revive an interest in one of the most fascinating aspects of pottery.

Fig. 7 Harvest jug, north Devon, 1792. This is a typical example of the strong and handsome sgraffito decoration of the north Devon harvest jug tradition. Jugs of this type would take almost a day to decorate. This one shows the royal coat of arms and a rhyme on a heart symbol. Harvest jugs were often made for farmers to supply beer to their men. Farmers also brewed their own beer which was not very strong — this ensured that the crop was harvested in time. Some men could drink as much as two gallons of beer during a day's harvesting, which doesn't say much for the beer, but a lot for the strength and stamina of the men!
Plymouth City Museum
Photo: John Baguley

Fig. 8 Detail of harvest jug.

Fig. 9 Dish by Ralph Simson, early 18th century Staffordshire, 16 inches. This dish has warped in the firing and has also been repaired after being damaged. It has a traditional border with a floral centre. Nothing is known about the four faces, although they do seem to be unhappy.
Plymouth City Museum
Photo: John Baguley

Fig. 10 Detail of the 'four sad men'.

Fig. 11 Border detail. Simson often spelt his name 'Simpson'. I wonder if he didn't leave enough space here to include the 'p'?

2 Clay, slips and glazes

Clay

The clay most commonly used for slipware is an earthenware body of a red or buff colour that will fire to between 1000° and 1120°C. White earthenware bodies are available, but I prefer the reds and buffs because these are the colours which were traditionally used by the 17th century slipware potters. Another reason why I like to use these darker bodies is that I often show a certain amount of the clay in the finished pots, and I am attracted by the warmth and richness of these darker, more earthy colours.

Slips

The most important point about decorating with slips is to ensure that the substance is of the correct consistency and has been thoroughly mixed. When I mix my slips, I usually pass them through a 120 mesh sieve twice. This helps the trailing to stick to the base slip. The whole point of having a slip that is very fine is that it will fit the body when being trailed, and has excellent adhesion. The finer a slip is, the higher drying shrinkage there will be; thus if the slip is finer than the body, there will be a tight fit. This only applies to air drying and not to shrinkage during firing which is another matter.

The colouring agents added to basic clay slip will play a big part in the final decoration of the pot. These are the more usual oxides, their percentages, and the colours that they will give in a white slip:

Chromium oxide: 1—5% gives grey-green
Cobalt oxide: 1—5% gives blue
Copper oxide: 1—5% gives green glazed, ochre unglazed
Iron oxide: 3—15% gives green to brown and black
Manganese dioxide: 5—15% gives browns
Nickel oxide: 2—5% gives grey-brown

The consistency of trailing slip should be such that when the full trailer is squeezed and a straight line trailed briskly, the slip should flow freely and smoothly. Two or three lines trailed in this way will soon indicate whether or not the slip is of the correct consistency. Before beginning trail decoration, I usually damp a throwing bat or wooden board and try out my slips on them before working on the pots. This gives me a good idea of how right they are to start work with.

It is advisable to mix slips for trailing thicker than for actual use in the trailer. The reason for this is that it is much easier to add a little water and make them more fluid than to have a slip that is too loose to start with.

I also find it a good idea to mix up trailing slip in 5 lb. batches (dry weight) and slightly thicker than is required for work. I add approximately $3\frac{3}{4}$ pints of water to 5 lbs. of dry materials. From these working slips I can mix to the exact consistency in smaller bowls. The advantage of this method is that the working slip can easily be adjusted.

For sgraffito and combing, the slip should be about the same thickness as for dipping pots. A slip that will be used for feathering should be slightly thinner, and one to be used for marbling should be thinner once again.

A standard base recipe for white slip is 50 parts china clay and 50 parts ball clay. To ensure a good fit of slip to body, I suggest an addition of 10—20% of throwing body to the base. This will also help the trailing slip to adhere to the ground slip.

A brown slip base would be 80% throwing body and 10—20% white slip. A black slip base is the same as brown with the addition of 4% manganese and 12% red iron oxide. Other colours can be obtained by adding colouring oxides as mentioned above to a white slip.

When the pot is nearly leather hard, it is dipped in a base slip. Immediately after this, it is decorated with trailing slip and then left until it is bone dry. If the workshop is warm — during or after a firing perhaps — cover the decorated pot with polythene as soon as you can do so without damaging the decoration. This prevents it from drying out too rapidly.

Common faults in trailing slips
One of the most annoying faults with slip trailing is that when drying, the trailed slip begins to peel away from the body of the pot. This is usually caused by the two slips having completely different shrinkage rates and drying far too quickly. Patience through the drying period is the answer to this. As I have already mentioned, a carefully sieved slip with some of the body clay in it will have a good compatibility with the body during drying. The

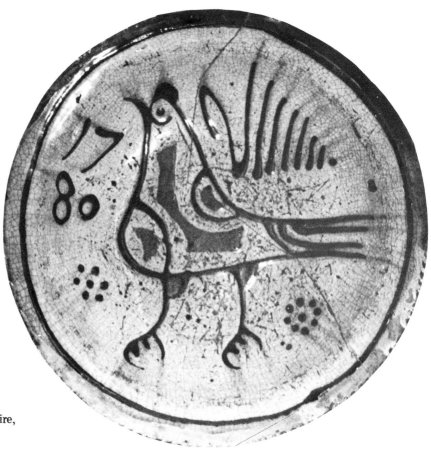

Fig. 12 Cockerel dish, Staffordshire, 1780, 13¾ inches.
Plymouth City Museum

22

other way of curing this annoying fault is to let the wet slip and leather-hard body dry out slowly so that they shrink gradually, and not too fast.

Slip may also peel away from the pot if the pot itself was too dry before it was dipped into the base or background slip. If this is the case, the water content of the base slip will be absorbed into the pot very quickly, making the base slip dry before the application of the trailed slip. This problem may be solved either by dipping the whole pot into water first, several times if necessary, or by spraying it with water from a plastic hand spray.

I have given here just two faults: these are the only two real ones. Experience and practice combined with the inevitable

Fig. 13 Detail of the Cockerel dish.

disasters will show you how fine are the lines between success and
failure when using slip in this manner.

Glazes

The purpose of glazing slipware is purely to put a very shiny clear
surface over the decoration on the body. In a glaze, roughly one-
third is water — the exact consistency depends on the biscuit
firing: if the pot is porous, the glaze needs to be thinner, but if it
is 'high' biscuit ware, the glaze should be thicker.

Glaze recipes

Here are four recipes as a basic guide. They are all for firing between 1020° and 1120°C.

Transparent leadless:

Borax frit 90
China clay 10

Transparent low solubility:

Borax frit 65
Lead bisilicate 25
China clay 10

Transparent low solubility:

Lead sesquisilicate 75
China clay 25

Transparent low solubility:

Lead sesquisilicate 66
Pot body 33

Fig. 15 Smoothing the base of a large platter with the thumb, in order to make trailing easier.
Photo: John Baguley

Fig. 16 Large thrown dish with
trailed decoration, 19″ diameter.
The design for the centre pattern is
taken from a plate excavated at
Donyatt in Somerset.
Photo: John Baguley

These will all give a very clear glaze. The addition of 1—5% red iron oxide will give more depth and a honey colour.

Here are two recipes for raw glazes:

Lead bisilicate 72
Red body 19
Flint 6
Red iron oxide 1
Iron spangles 2

Lead sesquisilicate 74
Red body 18
Flint 5
Red iron oxide 1
Iron spangles 2

These can be put straight on to a leather-hard pot, as well as on a biscuit-fired pot.

Fig. 17 Harvest jug, 14″ high, sgraffito decorated. The top verse is taken from a Chilean peasant tapestry and the bottom verse is from 'The Little Prince' by Antoine de Saint-Exupery.
Photo: John Baguley

Figs. 18 and 19 Harvest jug, 14″
high. This is thrown in two parts
and sgraffito decorated, A jug this
size will take almost a day to
decorate. The lion design is taken
from a Thomas Toft dish.
Photo: John Baguley

Fig. 20 5 pint teapot, sgraffito decorated. Both sides of the pot are dipped in white slip and the outer circle of dots is added. The rest is left to become leather hard before the sgraffito decoration is commenced.
Photo: John Baguley

Fig. 21 This type of crack usually occurs when the base slip is too thick. In this case, the jug was double dipped in white slip.

3 What to make

There are several methods of making pots suitable for slip decoration:

Slab pots

This method is not used to produce lots of pots, but for miscellaneous items. The first potters producing slipware by this method made things like money boxes, egg boxes, knife boxes and small toy cradles which parents would commission with their child's name written in slip round the side.

Flat ware

Plates, platters and dishes offer greater opportunities for decoration. They are also easier to decorate and there is no need to hold the pot while you are doing it.

Flat ware is thrown, usually on a bat — a circular piece of wood stuck to the wheel head with a layer of clay. The ware is decorated on the bat and after the slip has dried, the pot is removed from the bat, placed upside down and turned.

The thing to watch with flat ware is that you do not make the base of the pot too thin or too thick. Both these faults can cause cracking. You can test the thickness of the base by pushing a pin through while the pot is on the wheel.

Tall ware or hollow ware

The most important feature of decorating is knowing what you are going to do before you start. This is even more essential with tall ware because you must plan how you are going to hold the pot while decorating it. What I normally do is turn a little rim at the bottom of the foot. An alternative is to immerse the pot only about three-quarters of the way down in slip. In this way you can put your fingers round the bottom of the pot.

You must also consider in advance whether you are going to add spouts, handles or lugs. Any extra pieces should be sturdy and well applied to prevent the pot from losing its shape. Handles may also pull away from the pot and crack the rim if they are too wet.

Press moulding

There are two ways of press moulding a dish or plate. One is to lay the clay in a mould, and the other is to lay the clay over a mould so that you have either a concave or convex shape.

Both these techniques are probably quicker than throwing, although not so much skill is involved. Because of this, they

Fig. 23 Mould making: the prototype for the mould is placed on a piece of hardboard and surrounded by a frame which is loosely nailed together to allow quick dismantling. The seams of the frame are sealed by thumbing-in soft clay. The prototype and inside of the frame are then brushed over with soapy liquid. After the plaster has been poured into the frame and has started to set, the frame is knocked away to leave a square slab of plaster. The corners and edges can be scraped away to make the mould lighter.

could quite easily have been the sort of pots that apprentices would have made, ready for the master potter to decorate. Some of the older hump moulds that the clay was laid over had decorations cut into them so that the same pattern could be repeated inside each dish.

In my workshop we prefer to use the opposite type of mould — a press mould — and we decorate the pot while it is actually inside the mould. The first thing you will need to make is a pattern of the mould from which to make a casting. This is best done with some fairly stiffish clay which you can pat into the shape you want using a piece of wood. You can then scrape the clay into a smoother shape with a kidney or another piece of wood, smoothing it off finally with a leather or sponge until it is perfectly smooth because any marks that are left on this clay pattern will be revealed in the plaster.

The clay pattern should be made on a hardboard base because

Fig. 24 Cutting slabs of clay for small pressed dishes. This is a simple method of cutting slabs of clay to the same thickness. Two pieces of wood have grooves cut in them at even spaces. A wire is then slotted into the desired groove on either side and pulled through the slab of clay. The wire is then moved down a groove on either side, and the procedure repeated until the required amount of slabs have been cut.

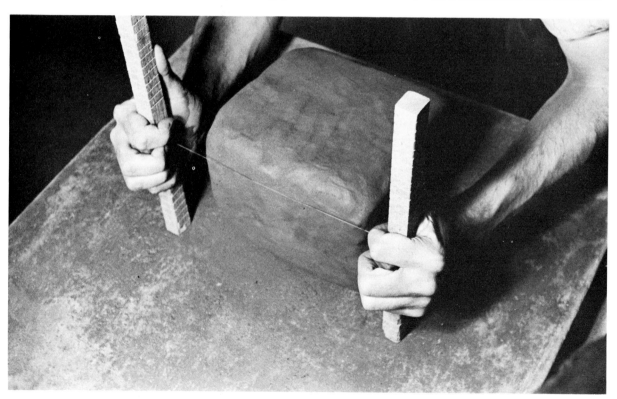

you will want to lift it once it is set. You can take as many castings off that pattern as you want moulds. A point to remember is that the clay pattern ought to be bigger than you want the finished pot to be because the pot will shrink in the fire. If you make a clay pattern, say, 12 inches square, bear in mind that it is going to shrink a ninth from that size by the time the pot is finished.

Once you are happy with your clay pattern, make a frame to go round it. You will need four pieces of 6 by 1 inch wood cut to whatever length the mould is. Thumb clay around all the joints to seal it completely. Before you pour the plaster into the frame, squirt some washing-up liquid all over the mould inside the clay pattern and brush it round the wood so that you have a very thin coating — like greasing a baking tin.

You can get potters' plaster, but we use dental plaster which any good builders' merchant supply. I mix the plaster in the

Fig. 25 Laying the slab of clay into the mould. It is then smoothed into the mould and the excess clay cut away as shown in the next section.

following way: I fill a large plastic bowl about two thirds full of water and slowly sprinkle the plaster into the water, a handful at a time. When a small mound of plaster appears above the surface of the water the mix is ready to stir. As soon as the mixture is of an even consistency it is ready to pour into the frame. Make sure that everything is well and truly covered. It is always best to make more plaster than you think you will need because it goes off very quickly and you have to work fast. Prepare everything in advance so that the tools you will need are around you.

Once the plaster has been poured, lift the wooden base up off the table and tap it a couple of times to make sure the plaster is packed down and the air bubbles are released. As you see it becoming solid — it looks rather like an ice rink — and the liquid area gradually disappearing, tap away the framework with a hammer. Quickly scrape round with a scraper and get all the excess plaster away. This will make your mould that much thinner.

Fig. 26 Preparation for a large pressed dish. The clay is being flattened on a damp piece of canvas — this helps it to spread more easily.

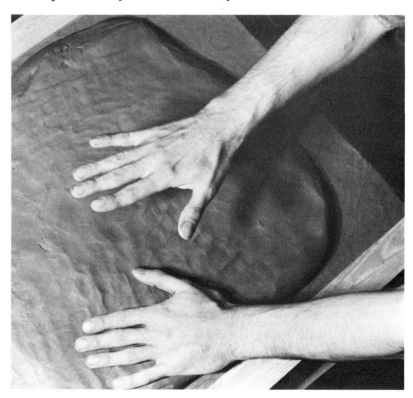

A nice light mould is about $\frac{3}{4}$ inch thick. Any thinner than that and there is a chance you will drop it or it will crack. If it is too thick, it is heavy to hold and when you pour the slip in, the weight combined with the clay already in there makes it all rather heavy to tip and pour the slip off.

The cardinal rule with moulds is always to get your pattern, or former, absolutely clean every time otherwise anything that is on it will carry right through to the mould.

Another important thing to remember is that after you have taken a casting from the clay pattern, before you put any new plaster back into the frame for another mould, you must make sure that all the old clay you have used to seal it with is removed and that it is re-sealed with fresh clay and everything is cleaned up. If you get any bits of dry clay in the plaster, it will affect the drying of the mould.

If you want to use moulds continually, you will find that they

Fig. 27 Working from the centre, the clay is rolled out in very much the same way as pastry. The two pieces of wood on either side are cut to the required thickness of the clay. It is easier to roll clay away from you than towards you, and when I have rolled out half the clay, I turn the slab round to face the opposite direction and roll the other half until it is the required size.

absorb moisture from the clay, especially if you are using slip as well. This means that the more you use them, the wetter they become and the longer the pots will take to dry in the mould.

A mould can be as big as you like. Size is governed by the capacity of your kiln and what you can handle in terms of weight. There is a traditional mould, called a boar's head dish, and its dimensions are 20 by $15\frac{1}{2}$ inches. This is a really big press mould dish to make.

For the smaller moulds which only need measure, say, 5 by 4 inches, you could try making several clay patterns, square or oval, building an individual framework around each of them, and then mixing up enough plaster to cast four or five moulds at the same time. In two or three sessions you could have as many as 15 moulds ready for use and when you come to actually use the

Fig. 28 Once the clay has been rolled out, texture can be added by placing some sacking or hessian on the clay and going over it a few times with the roller.

moulds, you can prepare enough clay to make 15 little pressed dishes — enough to keep you going for three or four hours decorating them.

Fig. 29 Peeling off the canvas. The clay is placed across the mould so that the textured side becomes the underneath of the dish.

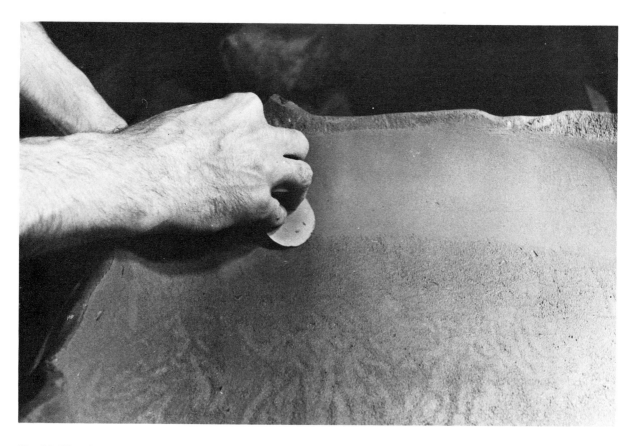

Fig. 30 The clay is smoothed into
the mould with a rubber kidney.

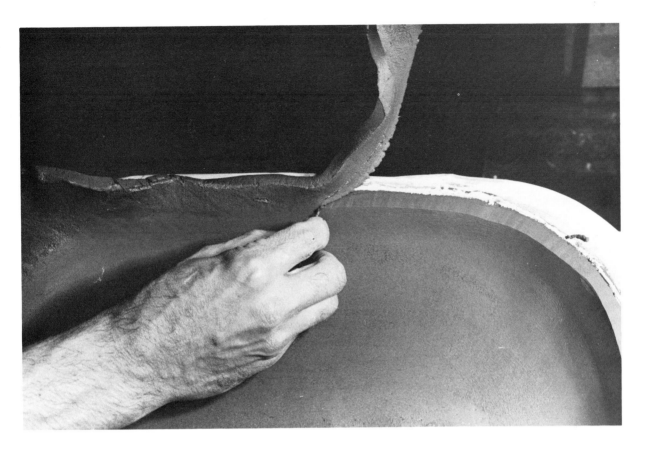

Fig. 31 Trimming off the excess clay with a pin. Note that this is done from inside the mould which helps to give a flat edge to the dish.

4 Decorating Slipware

As I said in my Introduction, the charm of children's work is in the spontaneity which comes from not having a technique. It is similar to the freshness of beginners' work. Children's naïveté combined with a sense of fun overrides the fear or hesitation about making a mistake.

There are dangers in acquiring technique. The resulting feeling of safety and false sense of security leads to unadventurous and less spirited decoration. Instead the result is tight designs which are technically competent, but the overall picture is dead.

It is interesting to look at the work of the Toft period in the 17th century (see Fig. 36). There are areas of the design that do not relate to the main subject — they are put in to fill up the space and there are often mistakes, but the overall decoration is full of spirit.

Posture

Just as a good piece of decoration should have a feeling of balance, so should one's posture while decorating also be balanced. The decoration should come from the whole body, not just from the wrist or forearm. A forced or uncomfortable posture over a long period of decorating will often result in tensions in other parts of the body, and this tension will be reflected in the decoration.

For example, if you were doing sgraffito on a jug, you might be inclined to hold the jug in your lap and stoop over it to decorate it. It would be less tiring to put it on a banding wheel on a table, almost at eye level, so that your back is straight. For slip trailing on flatware, you should build the work up on bats so that you are not bent over it.

You will know whether your posture is correct at the end of a long period of decorating. If you find you have aches and pains, during your next decorating session, pause occasionally and check the tensions of your muscles. It may help to gently stretch backwards for a moment or two.

Another instance when posture is important is when you are dipping pots in a bucket of slip or glaze. Bring the bucket up to waist level rather than stopping down to reach it on the floor. Improvise to suit yourself.

Fig. 32 White slip has been poured into this large dish and the first lines of brown slip are being trailed across it. Straight lines like these will give the beginner a feel for the trailer as well as enabling him to determine whether the trailing slip is of the correct consistency.

Fig. 33 The background slip being poured into a platter. This shows the creamy consistency of the slip.

Fig. 34 The ground slip being eased
around the inside of the platter.
Note how little is left to pour out.
You will soon learn just how much
slip a pot needs to cover it.

Fig. 35 Cleaning the rim with a
damp sponge. The pot is now ready
to decorate.

Fig. 36 (*opposite*) A Thomas Toft
dish, 17th century Staffordshire,
diameter $17\frac{1}{2}$ inches. The dish is
yellow glazed earthenware decor-
ated in brown and orange slip
with the famous trellis pattern on
the rim. *Victoria and Albert
Museum*

Fig. 37 Vinegar bottle by Clive Bowen, which I sometimes use as a bottle-type trailer.

Suggestions for designs

Look at traditional designs and patterns with a view to emulating them rather than copying them slavishly. This will help to bring about an understanding of the possibilities of slip decoration. Wherever possible, visit museums etc., and see examples of traditional slipware to get a more complete picture of the pots which photographs often cannot show. Work through patterns on pots illustrated in books — start by adding things and taking parts away.

A lot of the patterns that you find on early dishes, plates and jugs were taken from heraldry — the lion, the unicorn, oak leaves and so on (see Figs. 18 and 19). Inn signs were another source of decorative ideas, and humorous phrases or sayings of the day; for example, the 'We three fools' pattern which appears on jugs and flat ware. There is an illustration of two people, either sitting opposite one another at a table, or just standing side by side. Underneath is written 'We three fools', and the implication is that the third fool is looking at the two who are illustrated.

Fig. 38 The slip is poured in through the top, sealed in with a cork, and the flow controlled by placing a finger over the hole on the shoulder of the bottle. It is important to have the slip at the correct consistency and advisable to practise the pattern on a throwing bat, or something similar, before committing yourself on a pot.

Fig. 39 This type of trailer encourages you to trail patterns that have few long, continuous lines.

Fig. 40 The first line of the pattern completed.

Fig. 41 The second line of the pattern.

50

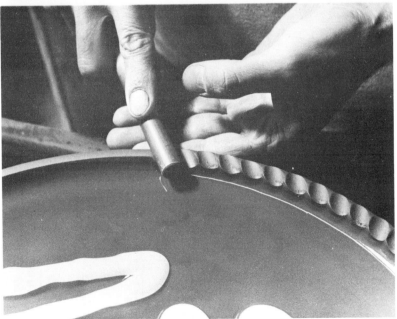

Fig. 42 The finished pattern. This is known traditionally as the 'Boney Pie' pattern due, I think, to its resemblance to the remains of a chicken, i.e. the ribs and wings.

Fig. 43 Crimping the rim.

Fig. 44 Detail showing where one line drags through another. When the trailing was completed, the pot was gently tapped underneath. This helps the slips to merge slightly and gives the trailed lines a nice fatness.

Fig. 45 The finished platter.

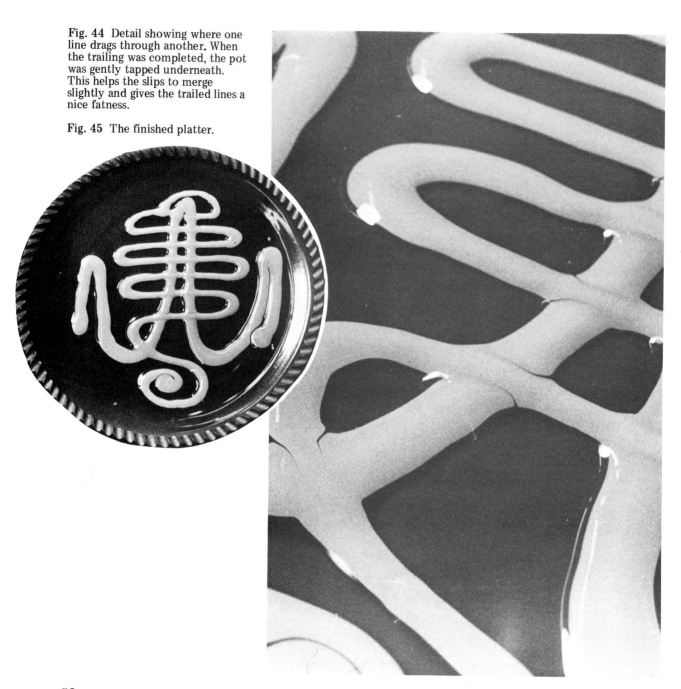

Fig. 46 Thrown jugs, 3-pint
capacity, with trailed decoration.
Jugs this size get heavy very quickly
if over-decorated. Note the feet
which offer something to hold
while decorating.
Photo: John Baguley

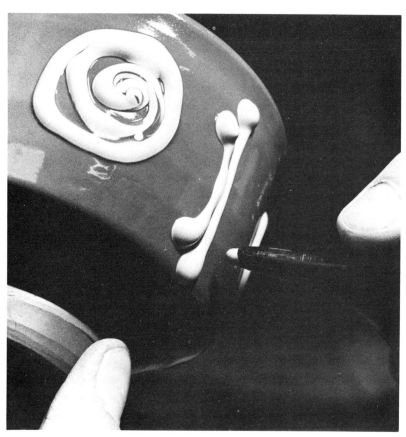

Fig. 47 Gripping the foot while decorating. Consistency of slip for trailing on tall ware is the same as for flat ware.

Fig. 48 Decorating a footed tea-bowl. Again, being able to hold the pot with ease allows you to give more attention to the decoration.

Fig. 49 Trailing decoration on a large platter. The ground is white slip, the trailing slip black.

Fig. 50 Filling in the diamonds with green spirals.

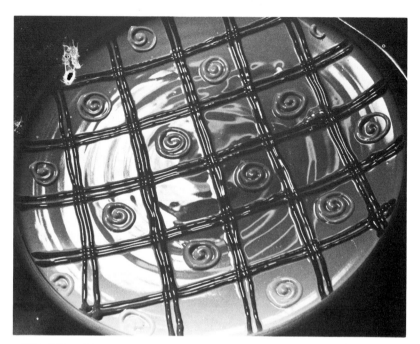

Fig. 51 The spirals completed.

Fig. 52 More diamond shapes being added to the pattern. Note the use of both hands on the trailer in these photos.

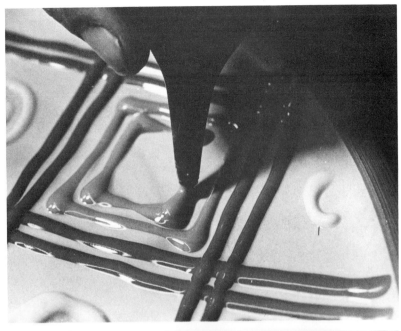

Fig. 53 Close-up of additional diamonds being trailed.

Fig. 54 The pattern is finished off by dotting the intersecting lines of black slip with white dots.

Verses such as:

'Within this jug there is a good liquor,
Fit for parson or for vicar,
But how to drink and not to spill
Will try the utmost of your skill.'

often appeared on puzzle jugs (see Fig. 4). These were jugs with holes cut in the sides below the rim, which prevented drinking in the conventional way. There was, however, a moulded pipe in the body of the mug, leading from the base of the mug, through the handle, and up to the rim. The trick was to use this pipe to suck up the contents of the jug, blocking any other outlets in the rim with the fingers while doing so. There was often a final twist to the puzzle, as many potters cut a small hole under the top of the handle, which also had to be found and blocked before drinking was possible.

Fig. 55 A smaller trailer being used to fill in an area with a slightly runnier slip.

Fig. 56 This shows the use of a glass pipette inserted into the end of a trailer. It makes a handy nozzle for fine lines and minute dots.

Fig. 57 Decorating a pot in its
mould. White slip has been poured
into the pot before trailing started.
Care must be taken, when pouring
the background slip, that the
pot does not drop out of the mould —
place your thumbs over the edge
of the pot as you pour the slip out.

Fig. 58 Marbling. White slip has been poured into the platter first. Then the coloured slips are super-imposed on each other with a trailer. The bottom of the pot should be tapped gently so that the marbling slips blend in with the ground slip.

Fig. 59 The finished decoration after the slips have been swirled by tilting the pot at different angles. Marbling never produces the same pattern. You can often seen images (faces, animals, landscapes) in a piece of marbled pottery. I frequently enclose a marbled pattern with trailed lines which are then dotted with white slip. I have also incorporated sgraffito with marbling when the pot is leather hard. Taoist potters enjoyed marbling as it reminded them of the ever-changing Universe with its constant flowing energies.

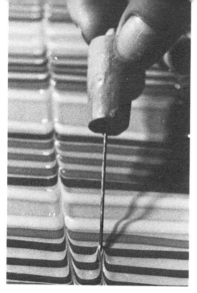

Fig. 60 Feathering. I use a pin instead of a feather. The point of the pin should be wiped every time it is drawn through the lines of coloured slips — this will keep the feathered lines fine and clean. You can achieve a variety of patterns depending on how the trailed lines are spaced, the combination of colours next to one another, and the directions in which the pin is drawn through the lines.

Fig. 61 Detail of the finished pattern.

Fig. 62 Sgraffito platter by Graham Stevens. The platter was coated with black slip and allowed to become leather hard. White slip was poured on to the black and left to become a little harder than leather hard. The dragon was drawn on to tracing paper first and then traced on to the pot with a sharpened piece of wood or a biro.

Figs. 63 and 64 (*overleaf*) Scraping out the lines after the tracing has been completed. A small, soft brush is useful to brush away the scrapings as you work.

Fig. 65 The completed design after all the lines have been scraped out.

Fig. 66 Scraping away the white slip to reveal the black beneath with a metal scraper. This has to be done very carefully or you will cut through to the body.

Fig. 67 Half-way stage before all the white slip has been removed.

Fig. 68 (*Left*). Close-up of the finished area around the dragon's head.

Fig. 69 (*Above*). The finished platter.

Fig. 70 Combing. Combed dish by Clive Bowen, 16 inches. Combing is a simple and direct method of decoration. Slip is poured on the inside of the pot and then swiftly wiped away with the fingers or a rubber kidney. A baby's rubber teat on the end of a stick can also be used.

Fig. 71 Platter with combed decoration by Clive Bowen. The immediacy of the design is a striking feature of Clive's work.

68

Fig. 72 Thrown dish, $15\frac{1}{2}$ inches. The black slip was allowed to become almost leather hard, then just the right amount of white slip to cover the bottom was poured over the black. At the same time, white slip was brushed over the rim. When both were a little more than leather hard, the pattern was drawn on to the white slip. The white slip was then carefully scraped away to reveal the black underneath.

Tools and seals

Improvise with what is at hand — knives, forks, sharpened bamboo or wood, hacksaw blades, etc. Of course, metal sgraffito tools can be purchased from the usual suppliers of pottery equipment.

You can also experiment with making seals carrying designs which can be stamped into pots. In previous times, these were used fairly frequently, but we don't often use them in my workshop.

Fig. 73 Some of the tools I use for sgraffito decorating.

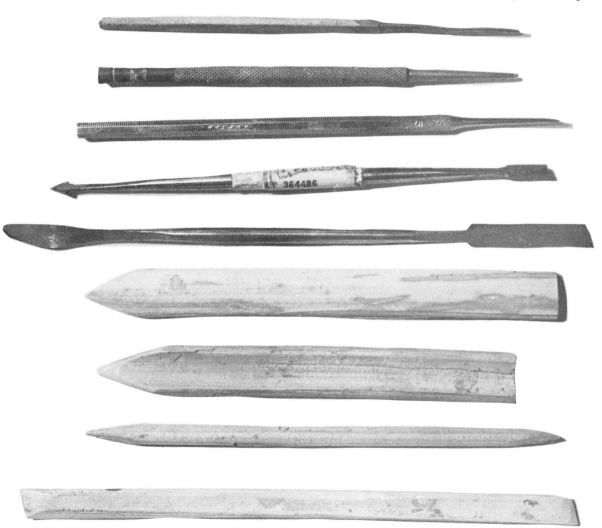

Fig. 74 'The Chef', sgraffito plate, 9½ inches. I enjoy what I call 'random pours'. I pour a small amount of slip into a plate or dish. I then ease it around the pot until it has spread out, and then I look at the outline to see what it reminds me of. In this case I noticed what looks like a chef's hat and then his nose. From that I gradually worked out the pattern in the photo.

Fig. 75 Thrown dish, $11\frac{1}{2}$ inches.
Sgraffito-decorated white slip on a
black ground. The honey glaze on
this pot gives the sun a warm,
glowing appearance.

72

5 Glazing and firing

Biscuit firing

If possible, pack pots to be biscuit fired into a warm kiln. When you have had a glaze firing or another biscuit firing, put the next batch of pots to be biscuit fired into the kiln immediately after you have unpacked the previous load. In this way, they will warm up before the firing starts. This allows any moisture that is still in the clay to escape. Otherwise, it can cause pots to crack.

Experience teaches us how best to pack a kiln and a good way to learn is by watching an experienced potter load a kiln and by unpacking it yourself.

It is very important to prop shelves correctly. Props must be level. Sometimes they get burrs on them from the shelf; chip these off or even them up with bits of clay. Another point is that three props placed in a triangular pattern are stronger than four placed in a square.

Flat ware is best packed with dots or pads of clay separating the pots — this, too, will assist the free escape of any remaining moisture in the pots, and is a better method than packing rim to rim. Remember that each clay dot should be directly above the one below it.

Most biscuit firings are at temperatures between $980°$ and $1000°C$. A rough guide to temperature climb is usually $100°$ an hour for the first six to seven hours. If the temperature rises too rapidly or cools too rapidly, it can cause dunting — hairline cracks as a result of moisture trying to escape too quickly. You would not normally notice them until glazing. When the temperature reaches $225°$ and $575°$, the firing should be slower, i.e. turn the

Fig. 76 This type of crack usually
occurs when the pot to be
decorated has not dried sufficiently.
I normally marble pots the day
after they are thrown.

Fig. 77 Cracks like this on the edge of pressed dishes are usually due to uneven drying, to rapid drying, or to uneven thickness of clay.

regulator down from high to, perhaps, medium. This is because the quartz in the clay body changes.

When the firing is completed and you are cooling the kiln, you should slow the process down again at 225° — but not at 575° this time. To cool the firing, open the kiln door very slightly, take a bung out, or open the damper and allow the kiln to cool slowly. If the kiln is densely packed with a lot of flat ware, it will take longer to cool.

Glazing

Always clean biscuit-fired pots. Make sure that they are not dusty because if they are, the glaze will not be absorbed fully. Also check that your hands are not greasy; if you have been using wax for wax resist and you start handling the pots, you can easily spread the grease around.

Before glazing make sure there is enough glaze to cover the tallest pot. Correct the consistency of the glaze — experience will teach you when this is correct.

Lead frit glaze particularly will need frequent stirring, but I like to stir all glazes regularly anyway. Once you start glazing, you build up a rhythm and stirring becomes part of it.

Start with the tallest pots first while you have enough glaze to cover them — obvious, perhaps, but this can be overlooked. For glazing large plates, a dustbin lid can be used as a glaze container. Being shallow and wide, there is plenty of room to dip the rim. To hold the dustbin lid steady while glazing, stand it on a bucket.

Lead glazes, being fluid, will often run down pots during firing if the glaze is applied too thickly or the pot is fired too high. Leave a suitable area unglazed at the bottom of the pot to guard against this happening and the pot sticking to the kiln shelf. Wipe lids and rims of pots well, otherwise they, too, will stick to each other.

Temperatures

The temperature at which a glaze reaches its maturity is critical, particularly with lead frit glazes. 10 to 15° either way will make a considerable difference and you must get the kiln temperature just right. Our glaze reaches its maturity at about 1100°.

I find that it is desirable to 'soak' the kiln at 1000° for ten

Fig. 78 Thrown dish, 20 inches diameter. The pattern is reproduced from Ralph Toft's Cruciform dish, now in the City Museum and Art Gallery, Stoke-on-Trent. It is a good example of a well-balanced pattern.

minutes. (This means keeping the temperature steady — as a cook would simmer a pan — for about 10 minutes and allowing it to rise gradually.) Between 1060° and 1100° I give the kiln a longer soak — just a gentle easing of the temperature for about an hour.

Common faults in slipware glaze firings

Crazing: this is caused because the body and the glaze do not fit. The body is underfired and has not shrunk as much as the glaze so the glaze has cracked. Crazing, however, can be used as a feature. Bernard Leach suggests soaking the pot in tea for a while so that the tannic acid highlights the crazing.

Peeling: this is the opposite of crazing. It is caused by the glaze having too much compression and lifting away from the body.

Bubbling: caused by overfiring or too rapid a firing. Perhaps the pot was too close to the elements in the kiln, or the kiln temperature was not cut back at the right time. If bubbling occurs, you cannot entirely remove the bubble but you can remove the sharpness with a carborundum stone so that it does not interfere with the handling of the pot.

6 Appreciation of slipware

It seems to me that the essential requirement of good slipware is flow. One should work towards patterns and lines that flow comfortably from the trailer. This is seen in the work of the 17th century potters, mainly because their slips were poured — not squeezed — from the trailer, and so had to form simple and direct patterns.

Try to discover for yourself when looking at a slipware pot which colours were applied first, where did the decoration begin, has anything been left out and could something have been added, but most of all, does it flow and have spirit?

The second ingredient is obviously colour. Earth colours are the ones most commonly favoured — browns, greens, blacks, yellows. Look for a balanced use of colour, and see if the glaze has given an extra depth to the colours. If the body shows through, look for the change of colour where glaze alone covers the body.

Finally, we come to the form of the pot, again with balance of flow and directness as the basic ingredients. Does the decoration fit the form and is it contained within and around the form? I once tried to imagine what it would be like to walk around the inside of one of my decorated jugs and see the decoration from the inside looking out. It was an entirely different perspective, similar to looking through stained glass windows.

I find another useful experiment is to look at the form of a pot and imagine it dressed as a person — is it over-dressed, dressed in the right places, do the 'clothes' suit the form and look comfortable on it? This is an easy exercise and soon gives an appreciation of what is correct for the form.

I would like to end by saying something about the commercial

Fig. 79 (*Overleaf*).   Author at work on a slipware dish in his studio. *Photo: John Baguley*

Fig. 80 Jubilee dish by the author commissioned for the Queen's Silver Jubilee 'Celebration' Exhibition at the Victoria and Albert Museum in 1977. The idea for the design was taken from an old 10p coin depicting the symbols of the four countries of Great Britain: the English rose, the Scottish thistle, the Welsh leek and the Irish shamrock.
Photo: John Baguley

qualities of slipware. Slipware cannot be decorated other than by the potter himself. No machine will ever be able to do it. This 'manual' method of decorating pottery means that it must assume a different selling price from pots that are not decorated, or are decorated in a less time-consuming style. For obvious reasons, industry prefers to leave all that to the craft potter, thank goodness!

I derive enormous pleasure and satisfaction from making and decorating a pot. I hope that readers of this book will have the same feeling for slipware pots, whether they make them themselves, buy them, or simply look at them in galleries and museums.

Where to see slipware

Most city museums will have a few examples of slipware. The larger collections can be seen at Fitzwilliam Museum, Cambridge; City Museum, Stoke-on-Trent; Victoria & Albert Museum, London; British Museum, London; Royal Albert Museum, Exeter. Make sure that the museum is open before you visit — many now close for one day in the week.

Galleries

London:
Boadicea, 42 Beauchamp Place, London, S.W.3.
British Craft Centre, 43 Earlham Street, London, W.C.2.
Casson, 73 Marylebone High Street, London, W.1.
Craftsmen Potters' Shop, William Blake House, Marshall Street, London, W.1.
Craftworker, 17 Newburgh Street, London, W.1.
            38 Castle Street, Guildford, Surrey.

Devon:
Cider Press Gallery, Dartington.
Windjammer, Salcombe.
'88', 88 High Street, Totnes.

My own showroom is at:
Barbican Craft Group Workshop, 1 White Lane, Barbican, Plymouth, Devon.

Appendix 1 Suppliers' list

UK Suppliers

Clays

English China Clays Sales Co. Ltd., St. Austell, Cornwall, do not supply customers directly with quantities of clay less than ten tonnes, but the following E.C.C. agents will deal in lesser amounts:

Anchor Chemical Co. Ltd., Clayton, Manchester, M11 4SR.

Fordamin (Sales) Co. Ltd., Free Wharf, Brighton Road, Shoreham-by-Sea, Sussex.

Somerville Agencies Ltd., Meadowside Street, Renfrew.

Whitfield and Sons Ltd., 23 Albert Street, Newcastle-under-Lyme, Staffs. ST5 1JP.

Watts, Blake, Bearne & Co. Ltd., is the other major ball clay and china clay mining company in the UK and they will supply quantities of clay above one tonne. Their address is:

Watts, Blake, Bearne & Co. Ltd., Park House, Courtenay Park, Newton Abbot, Devon TQ12 4PS.

Wengers, Etruria, Stoke-on-Trent, Staffordshire.

Ball clay BBV, earthenware clay, transparent glaze for earthenware.

Alec Tiranti, 21 Goodge Place, London W1, or 70 High Street, Theale, Berkshire. Grey modelling clay.

Podmore & Sons Ltd., Shelton, Stoke-on-Trent, Staffordshire.

David Leach porcelain clay, Duo-Clay, shiny transparent glaze for porcelain.

Deancraft Ceramic Supplies, Hanley, Stoke-on-Trent, Staffordshire. (Craft Division of Blythe Colours Ltd.)

High-firing body stains, *inter alia.*
Potclays Ltd, Brickkiln Lane, Etruria, Stoke-on-Trent, Stafford-
shire. Red clay and black clay.
British Industrial Sand, Etruria Vale, Stoke-on-Trent, Staffordshire.

Raw materials and pottery equipment
Podmore Ceramics Ltd., 105 Minet Road, London SW9 7UH.
Tel. 01—737—3636
The Fulham Pottery Ltd., 210 New King's Road, London SW6.
Tel. 01—736—1188
Ferro (GB) Ltd., Wombourne, Wolverhampton, Staffordshire.
Tel. 09077—4144
Harrison Mayer Ltd., Meir, Stoke, Staffordshire. Tel. 0782—31611
Degg Industrial Minerals Ltd., Phoenix Works, Webberley Lane,
Longton, Stoke-on-Trent, Staffordshire. Tel. 0782—316077
Wengers, Etruria, Stoke-on-Trent, Staffordshire.

US suppliers

American Art Clay Co. Inc., (AMACO) 4717 W. 16th St.,
Indianapolis, In 46222
Arch T. Flower Co. Queen St. & Ivy Hill Rd., Philadelphia,
PA 19118
Bog Town Clay, 75—J Mendel Ave., S.W. Atlanta, GA 30336
Castle Clay Products, 1055 S. Fox St., Denver, CO 80223
Cedar Heights Clay Co., 50 Portsmouth Road, Oak Hill, OH 45656
Ceramic Store, 706 Richmond, Houston, TX 77006
Clay Art Center, 40 Beech St., Port Chester, NY 10573
Cole Ceramics Labs, North Eastern Office, Box 248, Sharon,
CN 06069
Creek Turn Pottery Supply, Route 38, Hainesport, NJ 08036
Eagle Ceramics, 12266 Wilkins Ave., Rockville, MD 20852 and
1300 W. 9th St., Cleveland, OH 44113
Edgar Plastic Kaolin Co., Edgar, Putnam Co., FL 32049
George Fetzer Ceramic Supplies, 1205 17th Ave., Columbus,
OH 43211
Georgia Kaolin Co., 433 N. Broad St., Elizabeth, NJ 07207
Hammill & Gillespie, Box 104, Livingston, NJ 07039
Kick Wheel, 802 Miami Circle N.E., Atlanta, GA 30324

L & R Specialties, 202 E. Mt. Vernon, P.O. Box 309, Nixa,
   MT 65714
Leslie Ceramics Supply Co., 1212 San Pablo Ave., Berkeley,
   CA 94706
Metropolitan Refractories, Tidewater Terminal, So. Kearny,
   NJ 07032
Minnesota Clay Co., 8001 Grand Ave. S., Bloomington, MN 55420
Newton Potters Supply, Inc., 96 Rumford Ave., Newton,
   MA 02165
Paramount, P.O. Box 463, 220 N. State St., Fairmount, MN 56031
Rovin Ceramics, 6912 Schaefer Rd., Dearborn, MI 48216
The Salem Craftsmen's Guild, 3 Alvin Pl., Upper Montclair,
   NJ 07043 and 1042 Salem Rd., Union, NJ 07083
Sculpture House, 38 E. 30th St., New York, NY 10016
Standard Ceramic Supply Co., Box 4435, Pittsburgh, PA 15205
Trinity Ceramic Supply Co., 9016 Diplomacy Row, Dallas,
   TX 75235
Western Ceramic Supply, 1601 Howard St., San Francisco,
   CA 94103
Westwood Ceramic Supply Co., 14400 Lomitas Ave., City of
   Industry, CA 91744
Jack D. Wolfe Co., 724 Meeker Ave., Brooklyn, NY 11222

Appendix 2 Glossary

Ball clay A highly plastic clay, usually light in colour, which is the
basis of many potting bodies. Alone, it tends to be too fine and
slippery for use, but additions of sand, grog and coarser and
less plastic clays actually improve workability.

Base slip or **ground slip** is the first coating of slip the pot receives,
onto which other slips are applied — usually trailed.

Bat A common word with many meanings in the pottery. It implies
a flat surface and is used for kiln shelves, pot boards, detachable
wheel heads for repetition throwing, or for large pieces. A bat
is made from any suitable material which is slightly porous —
plain wood, chipboard and marine-ply are popular. If pots are
left on the bat to dry, they should first be separated from the
bat by drawing a wire underneath the pot. If used as a wheel
head, the bat is stuck to the wheel on a pad of soft clay.

Biscuit or bisque firing Firing unglazed pots. The most common
temperature to which pots are biscuit fired is approximately
980°C and it is a preliminary to glaze firing.

Boar's head dish A large, shallow rectangular dish with slightly
bowed sides, generally linear trailed and feathered.

Body Any clay, mixture of clays, or a mixture with other bodies.
Few natural clays are used alone but are blended together to
produce a mixture with specific qualities. There are as many
body recipes as there are potters. A clay is the natural product,
whereas a body is the result of man's technology. Since the clay
ceases to be clay and becomes ceramic during firing, the term
'body' is a useful one.

Boney Pie pattern A description loosely applied to a wide range of
freely trailed patterns said to have been formalized from the

left-over bones of a carved chicken on a dish. Other skeletal motifs have also been used.

China clay The purest natural clay. Its composition is approximately equal to the mineral kaolinite and it is therefore given the same chemical formula of $Al_2O_3 . 2SiO_2 . 2H_2O$. It is used in bodies to give whiteness, to clarify colours, and to control vitrification. In glazes it gives fluidity control at slop stage, viscosity control during the molten stage and adds stability to the final glaze. China clay is an essential ingredient in making porcelain body and bone china body. Because of its large particle size, the plasticity of china clay is poor.

Combing Decoration by wiping with a toothed or pronged instrument often made of wood or leather. However, the simplest combs are your fingers. Finger combing must be done very rapidly with the slip or glaze in an almost liquid condition.

Dots Small pads of clay or kiln props used to separate flatware during the biscuit firing.

Earthenware Pottery with a porous body which is waterproofed, if necessary, by a covering glaze.

Engobes Another word for slips.

Feathering or feather combing A method of decorating by trailing lines of slip on to a wet background slip of contrasting colour; the tip of a feather or another thin, flexible point is then drawn back and forth across the trailed lines.

Flatware Dishes, platters, plates, saucers etc. The term is used to distinguish them from holloware.

Foot In effect, a low pedestal which can be thrown on to a turned, inverted pot — usually a bowl shape — or cut from the surplus clay left at the base after it has been thrown. The proportions of a foot (its height, width and splay) can make or mar a form.

Galena glazing The practice of dusting finely pulverised or ground lead ore through a coarse cloth on to a damp pot, to which it adheres, forming a yellowish, slightly clouded fatty-surfaced glaze after firing. It is no longer used on parts of ware in contact with food and drink. Many early English slipware pots were glazed this way.

Glaze A layer of glass which is fused into place on a pottery body during firing. The glaze provides a hygienic covering on pottery. It is also decorative, providing colour, shine and textural contrast with the body. It increases the strength of the ware by the creation of a body-glaze layer.

Jewelled trailing The placing of dots of white slip along a darker line of trailing, often used as a surround for the motif.

Leather hard The stage which plastic clay reaches during drying when the clay particles are just touching, thereby giving a stability to the clay. The clay is stiff enough to be picked up without distortion, yet soft enough to respond to pressure. Leather hard is the ideal state for pots to be turned and have handles attached, for sgraffito decoration and for burnishing.

Lug A small handle or piece of clay on the side of a pot. Originally for suspending a pot on a rope.

Marbling Marbled slip patterns can be achieved by trailing different coloured slips on to a dish or pot, which is then either shaken sideways or given a sharp twist. The result can often produce surprising and beautiful patterns — if the result is not immediately attractive, continued shaking will only make it more muddy. Marbled bodies result from layering clays of different colours but of similar shrinkage.

Raw glaze A glaze which can be applied to a pot before it is biscuit fired, usually when the pot is leather hard, thus eliminating the biscuit firing.

Seals Most potters have their own stamp, or seal, by which their pots can be identified. Seals can also be used as an item of decoration. The design on a seal may be in relief or recessed. It can be cut directly into a plaster block from which casts can be taken.

Sgraffito From the Italian word 'sgraffiato' meaning 'scratched'. The technique of decorating by cutting, incising or scratching away a ground slip revealing the contrasting slip or body beneath. A speciality of the Pennsylvania German slipware potters. Also the North Devon potters specialized in decorating Harvest jugs in this way.

Shard Any fragment of broken pottery, often excavated near kiln sites.

Slabware Pots built up from slabs of clay. Leather hard slabs are cut with a knife, scored at the edges and luted together with slip made from the body clay.

Slip Powdered clay ground and added to water, then sieved to a creamy consistency. Coloured slips are made by adding small amounts of various oxides to the slip.

Slipware Lead glazed pottery, usually on a red body and decorated with slip by dipping, trailing, combing, sgraffito and feathering.

This honest and simple treatment of clay suited the temperament of English potters and resulted in some of the best peasant wares in the world.

Soaking The slowing down of the glaze firing, usually just before maturing temperature. This allows a steady firing during which the heat penetrates through the pots but does not rise too quickly.

Throwing The action of making pots on a rotating wheel head.

Trailing Decorating by means of extruding slip or glaze through a nozzle on to the surface of a piece of pottery.

Trellis pattern This is a border which is common on Staffordshire slipware dishes and it is thought to have been inspired by looking through a fence of upright palings at the shadows crossing diagonally beneath.

Turning Removing unwanted clay to achieve a particular form, thin a pot wall or create a foot, rim etc. It is usually done on thrown ware and at the leather hard stage. The unwanted clay is removed in a series of long shavings, using tools such as wire loops and sharp blades of metal or wood. The throwing wheel is often used in turning. The pot is centred and stuck to the wheel head with pieces of soft clay.

Wax resist Wax, either melted or as an emulsion, which is applied to pottery to prevent slips or glazes from adhering at that point.

Window dip A method of dipping a spherical pot sideways into slip, the result of which leaves a circle of slip on the side of the pot.

Appendix 3 Bibliography

Peter C. D. Brears: *The Collector's Book of English Country Pottery* (David & Charles, London, 1974)

Peter C. D. Brears: The English Country Pottery: Its *History and Techniques* (David & Charles, London, 1971)

Ronald G. Cooper: *English Slipware Dishes 1650—1850* (Alec Tiranti, London, 1968)

R. G. Hagger: *English Country Pottery* (Phoenix House, 1950)

J. H. Kelly: *The Hill Top Site* (Burslem Hanley Museum, 1969)

Dorothy Kemp: *English Slipware (How to Make It)* (Faber & Faber, London, 1954)

Bernard Rackham: *Catalogue of the Glaisher Collection in the Fitzwilliam Museum, Cambridge* (1935)

Bernard Rackham: *Early Staffordshire Pottery* (Faber and Faber, London)

L. M. Solon: *The Art of the Old English Potter* (E. P. Publishing Ltd, London, 1973)

Periodicals

Ceramic Review: 17a Newburgh Street, London W1

Ceramic Monthly: Professional Publications, PO Box 4548, Colombus, Ohio 43212 USA

Crafts: Crafts Advisory Centre, 12 Waterloo Place, London SW1Y 4AU

Craft Horizons: The American Crafts Council, 16 E. 52nd Street, New York, NY 10022 USA

New Zealand Potter: PO Box 12—162, Wellington, New Zealand
Pottery in Australia: Potters' Society of Australia, Turramurra,
New South Wales, Australia
Pottery Quarterly: Northfield Studio, Tring, Hertfordshire
Studio Potter: Box 172, Warner, New Hampshire 03278, USA

Index